Bathed in Abrasion

Bathed in Abrasion

Poems of Mid-life and Erosion

N. Thomas Johnson-Medland

Photos by Richard Lewis

For a dear couple. Lots of love.

RESOURCE *Publications* · Eugene, Oregon

BATHED IN ABRASION
Poems of Mid-life and Erosion

Wipf and Stock
An Imprint of Wipf and Stock Publishers
199 W. 8th Ave., Suite 3
Eugene, OR 97401

www.wipfandstock.com

ISBN 13: 978-1-4982-0127-8

Manufactured in the U.S.A.   10/16/2014

"It is those we live with and love and should know who elude us. Now, nearly all those I loved and did not understand when I was young are dead, but I still reach out to them.

Of course, now I am too old to be much of a fisherman, and now of course I usually fish the big waters alone, although some friends think I shouldn't. Like many fly fisherman in western Montana where the summer days are almost Arctic like in length, I often do not start fishing until the cool of the evening. Then in the Arctic half-light of the canyon, all existence fades to a being with my soul and memories and the sound of the Big Blackfoot River and a four-count rhythm and the hope that fish will rise.

Eventually, all things merge into one, and a river runs through it. The river is cut by the world's great flood and runs over rocks from the basement of time. On some of the rocks are timeless raindrops. Under the rocks are the words, and some of the words are theirs.

I am haunted by rivers."

—Norman Maclean
"A River Runs Through It"
University of Chicago press, 1976

"This majestic, ancient ice-flood came from the eastward, as the scoring and the crushing of the surface shows. Even below the waters of the lake the rock in some places is still grooved and polished; the lapping of the waves and their disintegrating action has not as yet obliterated even the superficial markings of glaciation."

—John Muir
"My First Summer in the Sierra"

Tom's Dedication:

For Thomas Howard and Richard Rohr and their lasting literary influence on my life and pen. Thank you, both!

Rich's Dedication:

To my wife, Vivian, who affords me far more patience than I deserve. Thanks for the countless hours you spend waiting on the sides of numerous trails while my artistic vision evolves.

Cape May Beach

Introduction

Around the age of thirty five, people tend to notice that they are not the same as they had been. They sense the world is a moving and a shifting place. Things that they were able to attain earlier in life require a lot more focus and attention once they cross this age line. By this age folks have experienced multiple losses in their lives, a few deaths, several career upsets, and establishment and reestablishment of major relationships.

Life becomes less stable in our perception because we learn to notice things from a higher vantage point. We view it over an expanse of time and space and see it in a more "whole" view. When we have aged to this place in life, we have a whole series of years—thirty five to be exact—that we can compare to and against each other. The vantage point of age helps us to interpret cause and effect in a whole new way.

There will be outliers for this process, as with every other theory and truth. There are always people that are on the curve of an idea or issue. But, just look around you. Things slow down and take more time when you get older. Most people catch onto this.

I know that I saw some shifts in perception, because at thirty five my parents were much older and the slowing down I experienced was partially built on top of the slowing down that they experienced. The processes of those around us impact our own.

It was around this age that I began to have an affinity toward certain geologic landscapes in life. I returned to a fascination with alluvial fans, and escarpments. I found the way rock changed from one form to another peaked my interest. How one thing could start out as wood and then turn to rock amazed me. That rivers changed their shape over centuries was provocative. One thing lead to another and I knew I was in those things somehow. The images and explanations of land and rock formations held my attention for a long time—it still does.

I started to feel the shifts and changes in the natural world as somehow emblematic and iconic of the life I was living. I somehow was a part of the shifting of matter in the universe of energy and form.

I felt I could live into things I was seeing. It became a way of finding and understanding my personal meaning. I could feel how the changing course of rivers held my cells in some kind of regard and relationship. I knew that the alluviating debris that is sloughed off a mountainside bespoke my own condition of giving away and losing what was in my me.

I sensed that mountains being made low and valleys being filled up was not just a principle of geologic time, but was close to the meaning of all things and the sort of change that space/time would visit upon them. Dimensions and states are constantly being altered and I could feel that dance of change in my soul, in my every cell.

I had spent a lot of time in the wild. All my life. It was not unusual for everything in me to reach out and participate in the universe at large—that feeling of being content and blissed out by nature—being at one with that over there and this in here. But, I noticed a shift. Erosion, entropy, and abrasion were things that began to resonate with my me—the whole of my cell body, mind, and soul. They made sense one day, like they were somehow me.

I found decay not so unusual. The way a tree slowly unburdens itself by becoming the earth on which it lay was sort of quaint and expected. The protuberance of fiddleheads from leaf matter, the growth of fungus on tree rot seemed to have a selective sense of practicality and design. That things fell apart started to become an intuited reality and comfort.

+ + +

Something in me turned around forty. I started digesting the Civil War for breakfast. It was if I could not get enough. Somehow, the turning of one part of a thing against another part of that same thing was understandable. Reminded me of cancer cells and the body. Having been in hospice since I was thirty six that made sense. Sometimes pieces of oneself revolt against the main; they retaliate against the whole. My parents' divorce added hues to that idea.

Watching people in groups since I was twenty also gave me reason to believe that Civil War might just be a usual way for people to grow as a community or social organism—a culling of the herd mindset. It just seemed natural. Not necessarily glorious, but natural. Some things just need tidying up a bit.

The two were linked. The wild and the war. I had not made the connection, though. I saw how atrophy of will and purpose may lead men to kill that which is also themselves. I knew that there were things that took over organisms that set them on processes and cycles that seemed in contradiction to growth and homeostasis. But, watching how things fall apart in the woods, and seeing those boys decomposing on the battlefield may have been the greatest neural pathway that I was able to light up. Couldn't escape decay, couldn't escape death, and couldn't escape unravelling social order. And then, I made the connection.

The connection came in my writing. I began to see the geologic landscape with battle overlays. I could sense a charge over a bluff that was outlined with crenulations of alluviated matter and debris. I listened to the talk that must have gone on in the countless tents and heard the winding of rivers through a lowland descent—busting the ambling and sidewinding banks when a flood was forced upon the basin. I saw a little gully on the side of a stream bed and I knew it had been a hiding space for a young soldier with a gun.

All of the sudden the phlox and lavender were not just perennial plants but sentinels of remembrance that pushed themselves out of the ground in response to the aeons of death and decay that had nourished their very roots. Nature was a vibrant retelling of the story of living and dying. All life that fell to the ground got born anew in the rivulets of daffodils along the field. Not one thing escaped being used for some other thing. That is poetry, that is geology, and that is war.

It was clear that although I could see conflict and battle on the landscapes all about, there were battles and conflicts going on within me that I had no account of. Just simply because we give our nod of assent to something that is going on around us, does not mean that we are indeed in agreement with its coming to pass. Think of all the compromise you learn to stomach as you age.

We may be in disagreement with a thing and yet unable to recognize the deeper truths and lineaments of our disgust. We may be unable to rally words to support a hunch. We may not even know that that inkling down within is a hunch of aversion. As complex and vast as the heavens are above us, so within lives equal panoplies of mystery and awe. We are—all of us— broader than the heavens.

+ + +

Regardless of how I feel about it, things wear away. The processes of the universe go about their way without consulting my belief for acknowledgement and approval. I am really not that critical in the overall scheme. And, when things wear down, there is a smoothness that time buys for them. They become somewhat easier to look at.

+ + +

Suffering eats at a man. In many ways, suffering is a coming to terms with the way things are and are becoming for us—in antithesis to the interior sense and desire of how we wish things would or were to be. I long for something I may not have; and, the absence of that which is longed for is measured in increments of suffering. It is good to note that desire and longing are seeds for what often turn out to be suffering situations.

But, far from wrong or negative, the desire and longing themselves can be the pool of drive that help us to find sweetness and flavor in life. Without them, aspiration is dead; with them we will surely feel the sting of suffering as well. Everything grows toward wholeness amid the soil of suffering, bliss, and yearning. Eventually, everything that is falls apart—and this is a layer of suffering in its own right. Trees, countries, families, marriages, rocks, buttes, and mountains, they all come undone. Suffering.

The center does not hold. Things fly apart. Centripetal force moves things away. When you can arrive at a place of being able to acknowledge that "pieces of you are flying away from your mass—from your center", then you have taken one great step forward to say, "there is me, and there is NOT ME." Once that line has been crossed, then there is battle with whether to take those things back into yourself, or count them as lost. Do we strive for unification, or learn to languish and grieve what we could not hold onto forever?

At some point in this wrestling with ontology and etymology the core sense of self comes into question and either you land on the side that says I and Thou, or you land on the side that says Everything Belongs. Either way, battling centripetal forces is costly and tiring. The ardent warrior knows when to accept ground that was lost. In it, he finds a solace of all that has survived.

Things change. How will we be through that coming and going? Will we survive or will we decay? Will we be diminished by the removal of things from our me? It is hard to know what comes next, so trusting into the taking away of something must be based on large more all-encompassing views of life based on vantage points beyond the immediate. But, even in the going away of things, is anything really ever lost?

+ + +

Water has a captivating allure. Its simple coursing and ambling delight can draw you out of the deepest stupor of unaffectedness and delay. It can make you to take firm stock in the value of life and the very transient nature of being flesh and bone. In a way that is its power to erode; it takes away an indifference that comes with a stalwart weathering of sorts. It can move things that are too large to move; it can wear down the things that seem almost eternal.

I have often felt the pull and tugging of the power of water on the heart and mind. Standing in a stream—up to my knees in water—there is something constantly asking me to leave myself and head to the zenith of the flow. Move out and away from the me. It is often the call of all of nature. Come out of yourself and enter the flow. What would it be like to be under that falls? How would I find myself to be if I were just around that bend?

The Anglo-Saxon bardic literature is filled with escapes into shape-shifting and transmutation of form. At first glance, the uninitiated would suspect some supernatural interruption of the mundane huggermugger of the daily grind. But, this a not the case. Anyone versed in spending any small amount of time in the out of doors knows how everything in the ken of your view is inviting you to come out and play. Leave the confines of your own skin and dance with mirth and abandon in the wiles and the ways of the earth kingdom.

It is the great Taliesin that again and again becomes a trout, or a roebuck, or a hawk. He climbs from the stream, to the land, and to the sky in instantaneous flashes and blinks of the eye. You can feel this same sort of elevation of the soul when you peruse a stream, a landscape, and the sky. The eye carries the heart from one place to another. And with it, if you feel for it deeply, you will find new vistas of feeling and emotion, of knowing and understanding.

This sort of elevated aspiration to the grand can only come if one is able to leave the daily behind. You could conceivably head out into the wild with a heart and mind filled with bills, and tasks, and machinations of social greatness. Filled with these things, you will never be enfleshed in the change and elation of nature. You must allow the daily grind to be eroded enough to allow the "pristine nature of being" to fly through and out of yourself, you must let go enough to become. This eroding is a soulful abrasion of all that is a barrier to human growth. It is a goodly undoing of impediment and confinement. It is the abrading of the soul into freedom.

+ + +

This, of course, is all a matter of perspective. And, of course, that is exactly how I view the abrasion of things in life. One has the option to see that which is carried away as a natural and helpful process, lending to the development of the plot. Or, one can view it as conflictual series of sub-plots running against the grain of the plot.

    If people see that which is carried away as detrimental, then they will ache in the absenting of things from their whole. I think most of our lives are a wrestling with these ideas. We drift back and forth between the poles of belief until we are able to settle in to one way of being. This takes a lifetime. In the end, I believe that leaning into surrender and release will be the triumphant one in the realm of the emotions and efforts. That ultimately, yielding is greater than acceptance, it is the way of life and growth. It is our tininess of minds that keeps us from seeing fully into the bloom that comes from a black-hole. It is only discovered on the other side of annihilation— Rumi knew this.

+ + +

Now 53, I am standing midstream in the abrasive forces of life. Erosion and entropy are all around. Failure and incompleteness are things I now learn to manage. Suffering is like breathing. Longing is like dreaming. If compromise and disappointment have a home it is midlife. And yet, in spite of these massive forces attempting to wear down the very vitality that sustains my life, I have come to abide in the fact that life is amazing, and wonder filled and awesome. My place in the cosmos is full of joy. My island is hope. My vision is beauty. Let the forces do their best to wear me smooth. For, in it I find great refinement and grace.

+ + +

And so, let us swim among the abrasive forces of life: wilderness, war, suffering, water, they are all a part of the poems of our lives. Watch for the meter of erosion and decay. Listen for the sound of sloughing off. For, surely as all things decay, they are changing shape into a new becoming. For nothing is lost; everything belongs.

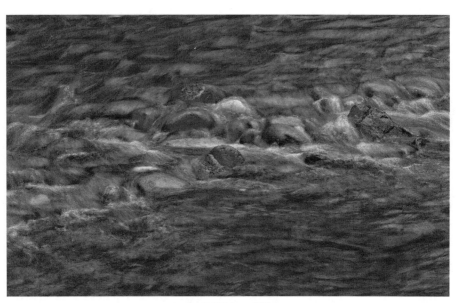

Dark Waters, TN

The Poems

Escarpment

Some things wear you down;

a deep aging in your center,
an erosion of your soul

or maybe your heart.

It does not kill you,
but
it lays you bare,
open,
exposed.

This wearing down becomes clear
in the middle of life. One thing
comes along: a death, an accident,
a final straw that lights the mind's
sky, and all at once you
see what has been there all along—
that which has undone you—that
which has worn you away.

There it is.
And,
don't be shy,
it goes
against your earliest hopes, your
youthful ideals, and your grandest
theories. There it is,
a piece of you, one
that was left exposed
as if it were something new.
Like the rock held deep
in the earth, erosion,
time,
alterations pull the dirt
from all around the stone.

They pull the dirt
from this piece of you
they move the pebbles from
your side, they move the sand from behind
and you are revealed
by the violence of change.

This need not be horrid violence—
the great unleashing slide of
the glacier as it tears away from it's
century nest,
pushing
with a crashing speed.
A simple negotiated shift
is enough. A slow movement
back and forth, to and fro,
earth and weather,
drifting and decaying and
just simply washing away.

Some things wear you down;
a deep aging in your center,
an erosion of your soul
or maybe your heart.

Childs State Park Waterfall, PA

Strata

Our days are made of
varied ages and
altering composition;

layers of change through
out time and space.

To feel the changes
that have been made
does not require
the minds' knowing alone—of where
one thing ends and
another begins.

Nor is the
heart's feeling enough.

We need
a gut that senses change,
an intuition that
senses the shifting
plates and layers
of life. We need a
heart and a mind that will trust
the gut.

In us,
down deep and beneath
are movements we cannot see,
upheavals we will never behold,
shifts we cannot know will come.

We can sense them.
We can lean forward at
the first stirrings—bend into
them and suppose or
hunch.

Strata

It is the gut that notices
this larger terrain—this immense
sliding. It is the gut that
feels its way through changing
landscape.

The eye may not see, the mind,
it may not know, the heart may
not feel, but the gut senses.

The gut holds on
to shudders and rumbles. The
gut explores valleys and
hills, the faults and
plates of the
topology of our lives.

The gut knows nothing
of fur and feathers,
of brocade and silk.
It holds no hope in the fine
and the soft: amid
the smooth and refined.

The heart and the mind,

they loll themselves
to sleep
in the finery. Casting their
eyes on the silt and lace
of the low grade terrain;
feeling for a faint
interior pulse that they
cannot know.
Our days shift and move
without regard for the mind's
vigilant hope for reason, and
the heart's need for rhythm

and rhyme. Things
move about without warning.

I cannot hope to see
that plate raised up above the others
or that one dropped down below.
The gut knows disturbance:
turbulence is its language—
and it knows it well.
My gut feels them:
a jarring drop or jolting
rise is measured for sure in
the gut. The heart, the heart
reaches out and feels
through the layers of space
and time for the shifting
and the rolling forces.

We no longer see—the
sorrow and the joy
that arrives from change
ushered in on the current
of the hummingbird's wing
at noon day.
Layers of life
that we cannot see.

We are piles of layers
within the twist of time
and the stretch of space;
the spray of the wave
and the stir of air.

We hold on amid
our lack of ingenuity;
we dream on despite our
innocence of any true power.
Sensing only the dark,

Strata

feeling only the layers
of our piled past,
we hope against hell that our
heart and our mind have
listened well and found
what is true, what is sure—
what the gut has to offer.

Alluvial Fans

Fans spread out at
the base of the hills
the base of our days
escarping debris
deposited over time.

The force—
always down
hauls all sorts of silt
from the face of the
highlands to the foot
of the lowlands.

Down,
always down falls
all that has died,
all that has decayed
and lost its grip.
It falls and is
washed away.
Are the things we
love really lost or
are they moved—
down, always down—
away to the pit
of our erosion.

Those pieces that have
washed away—
our youth,
our trust,
our freedom to be naïve.
Are they gone or
simply out of sight—
reaching out from
the basin of our days.

Alluvial Fans

The nutrients and minerals
from the mountain
seed the basin
in a downward rush.
The mountains and
the hills laid low—a time
cast collaboration of the
prophets and erosion;
everything leveled.

Fingers of the mountain
stretch out
hoping to pull her along
the earth,
to widen her presence
along the surface. We
grow like this. All that runs
off of us produces chains
and foothills. Our life
touches another by the
buildup of silt and alluvial
wear. It moves away from
our core. Then, lifetimes
later, the foothills of our
days spawn foothills and
are themselves carried away.
All things become one
as the work of time
spreads out the mountains,
bringing them all to the ground,
to the earth from which
they came.

The mountains and the hills
laid low.

Dunfield Creek 2, NJ

Moon-Bow

There is some grief in everything;
even in the light.

A time when darkness is shrouded
by a hard glow silvery moon.

A smile in the presence of the dead.

Do we not feel a damp and subtle
angst and dissuasive play of emotion;

a simple collaboration with consent.

Slowly eroding the fullness of the dark;
light shines,

with varied dappled-ness among the tears a mourning
earth sheds.

Light saturates our bones
'til gladness converts the pangs hidden behind

a gallant exposure to erosion
and all that seeks to wear us down.

This simple tableaux of diminished energy
and satisfied passivity.

The moon gives itself to the river's tears -
and darkness radiates immense and colorful
bliss.

Across the River - Somewhere in the War Between the States

I do believe
that
as I had looked
across the river -

toward the embankment
on the other shore -

I do believe
that
I had seen
the silvery-blue
glint of steel
hidden in the
soft and simple
branches of that
shrub -

of that Missouri
gooseberry.

I know
that,
that steel
was a piece
of the conflict;

a piece of our
fratricide;

a piece of the
war between the
States.

It hung there
still as the
fragrance of
the flowering milkweed.

The flower's sweetness
suspended in the
rising –

heated moisture
of the sun on earth –

the sun on soil.

The steel suspended
on the anticipation
of the darkness
of night.

There comes a wearing
down on me; a wearing
down of waiting

for the enemy
to strike.

It is a wearing down
in my center.
It is a wearing down
in my being.

Is this how
I shall go mad;

sitting here picking out the
steel from among the
shrubs, from among the flowers;

slowly taking away my
thoughts, my reason, my soul
- my very desire to live.

Ants carrying their eggs
away –
to God knows where.

This is how a river cuts deep;

this is how a rock is smoothed;

aeons of flooding
and glacial drag.

My grandpa told
me this would come,
if we spent too much time
facing into

the bloody
and bruised business
of fighting our own -
of killing our brothers.

Water itself can wear
things smooth. It
just takes time.

And me, here on
this side of the river; and,
perhaps
only one battlefield
away from death –

the Great Abrasion –

of looking into
The Mystery.

Me, three years
into this war, I
am worn down smooth.
This constant conflict
of fighting and death
has taken all the roughness
from the edges
of my days.

I am not here
aeons to stand the
glacial tears and torrential
floods of sand and stone
on rock and earth.

But, I am bathed in
abrasion.

And, if I live to see
an end to this bitter anguish
and everlasting conflagration,

then I

shall have no
roughness left
in me. I will only sit
and stare - hollowed
out by what this
freedom has come
down to. I will have
no words because of
all that has just

transpired.

Such Fondness in a Leaf

Such fondness in a leaf,
such familiarity in a flower,
such simplicity in the fog –

forcing my gaze down;
here, right here
in front of me. NOW.

I cannot see beyond
the forty paces
enshrouding me
with a dense wall of
droplets of moisture.

Who knew the fog
to be my master –
telling me what to do
and keeping me
from others.

Who knew the weather
to guard my heart –
keeping me
close to the things
that nurture
me.

There is no sound
to the tears the night sheds
but it should
meet some sort of resistance.

The rain needs
a leaf,
a pond,
a stone
to give it voice.

Such Fondness in a Leaf

Think on this,
it is only by virtue
of its volume and its speed
that you can hear

the increase of the showers
as they land upon the lake.

It is what stops them
or slows them down
that echoes the singing
of the raindrops.

How droopy is the pine
along the path laden
with the early

morning showers.
She holds the rain until she
can hold it no more. She
sets it free

in measure

to her tolerance.

Ricketts Glen 03, PA

One Is Enough

The principles of
abrasion are
miniscule
and often
nondescript;

flotsam and tiny
grains of sand

can easily
wear away
a mountain
of angst
and even one
of strong
and
lingering hope.

It is all
dependent on the
way you hold your
face against the
change;

the way you
lean into the newness
of each and every
increment of time –

a time that goes
on endlessly in its
devotion and focus
to carrying away
with it
pieces of the
you that

you had clearly
thought

immovable and
relentlessly
eternal.

Safe.

Solid.

Not so;
oh, not so.

It is only
one ray of
a sunbeam
that feeds
arboreal growth;

one grain
of sand
on the shore
that washes over –
always over –
the stones
smoothed in
their stillness
and sitting
on the river
basin floor;

one snaking
curve in the
ambling river
to yield itself
and all its
water

crashing; tumbling
over the edges

into places the
mind of man
had hoped and planned
it should not go.

It is in one small
instance of time;
one small
and whispered secret
of a sentence about the
full and summary
meaning of all life
and its intricacies
that little bits
of nothing
carry away the
all and everything.

It is in that
small and simple
place on
space and time
that everything
is nothing
and everything
at once.

A sassafras
creeps itself
deeper into dirt;
deeper into earth-soil
and finds contentment
in the slow moving
growth of roots
that crack a rock

with dank and loamy
root-beer aroma.

A clover rises
to the sky
showing off
its glorious purple
tendrils filled
with fragrant sweetness.

The fulcrum
of the entire cosmos
is levered against
the infinitesimal
wispiness the
soul and its
simple
ineffable nods
of the affirmative.

An "ah-ha"
can stretch
itself
into the furthest
reaches of the galaxy.
The smallest
of hands can
obscure the
greatest of mountains.

Quasars are built
on the same stardust
that supports
the data for this very
thought –

this one
right now –

One Is Enough

and the
mitochondria
on the end of
a lash
just below
the eye.

One
is
enough.

Ringing Rocks Falls, PA

Dendrites

Sometimes,
one thing reaches out
across what seems to
be an endless divide –

a space that stands between.
The distant thoughts
of silent aspirations
that a mother will
not voice
for her daughter
or a father for
his son
until it is
too late.

These spaces need
to find an intrusion
of immense compassion
and dilapidated ennui
that cannot keep the edges
abruptly and obscenely clear.
This one, here;
that one, there.

There is a headward
erosion that interrupts
the simple dendric flow
of water down
and
away.

It is an erosion on
the back piece of land
between two rivers
that will divert
the water's flow

in an opposing direction.

Some places give water
the special gift to flow
up and against
what seems to be a natural
lay.

The force –
special to these places,
alone –

causes water to push out
and back up –

from one basin to the
next.

At some point;
somewhere
along the climb,
the headward waters will
cause the rivers to merge –
draining both into one.

The Fianna cut across
the boundaries and the boarders
layed out neatly as
routes, and paths, and
runways of a people;
invading spaces that
may or may not have
been open for
the changing of routine.
This band of
Irishmen kept things
in order and
under control

Dendrites

amid times and
tides of quick-swell
and turbulence –
when hegemony was king.

Why should water lack
a way to move
against the accepted
direction and
flow?
And yet,
it could be denied
that water shapes the land;

shapes the way the earth
lays itself out around
its own core.

This denial
would only be
the sensibility of one
who has seen only days –
and perhaps only decades –
of water's way with

soil and stone.
For, the one
who takes a longer view –
the one with sensibilities
of a vantage point of epochs
and eras –
the alluviation of
a weekend is
nothing like the
disintegration of a mountain

over time.

What Does the Water Wash Away

What does the water
wash away, what does it
take that is not brittle
lacery and encrusted
crystals showing
off residues of sleep
and pollens trapped
in the corners of my eyes.

Ringing Rocks Falls 2, PA

It Wears Down Mountains

It wears down mountains,
and I have seen it take
pieces of who I am holding onto.

I have not yet seen it take
my hope; this alluvial force
from the clouds and the skies;
this force from the showers of gravity
and the spinning galaxies
of space and interstellar matter.

It can move
whole cities into the sea,
but I have not felt it
rob me of any joy – this
energy given
to attachment and
aversion and the
falling of the rain.

I have watched it move
away from me portions
of the things I had felt
were monumental limbs
of the self.

Seeing the muddied
pieces of the river
reminds me there
are variations on the
currents I believe I know.

Simple lines I
had memorized to
write once I returned
to the confines of my
muse.

It Wears Down Mountains

There are knowings of the
water's pull I have no knowing
of – nor even an inkling.

There are days I awake
feeling I have lost some
thing I cannot name. Perhaps a
way to put on my socks
or gather lint from my pockets –
but, it might be more like
the ability to remember some
thought that is stored in an
ancillary set of axons on the
backend of an occipital lobe
I thought would never weather.

The hardness of bedrock
and river rock is carried
away as the sun and moon and
earth all turn on the axis they
have named as their own –

how is it I thought my holding
of memory and place would
be screwed down with the
force of some interior gravity
and everlasting fixity.

Dis-integration
is the way
ALL
things go.

All things.
We spend our days
between the holding on
tightly and the watching
of it being carried away.

It is this that tires us;
it is what wears down
mountains – within
and without.

Those Promontories

To wear down those promontories –
the ones inside that are decked
with boughs of hope and glee –
takes a concerted act of heinous
hatred; an anguished anger
against
the core
of a person's being.

Abraded by Glacial Drag

If you have not stood
on ground
abraded by the massive
momentum and force
of glacial drag –
glacier over rock,
and glacier over mud –

you have not felt
the infinitesimal smallness
in the center of your chest
that calls you to the knowing
that you are naught but dust.

It sounds so riven –
that falling sound of water into
a gorge far greater
than its course.

Endless Reaching Darkness

If there was
a moment through which
the LIGHT could escape
into the endless,
reaching darkness of
intuition and desire,

it would be now.

If there was a
crevice through which
the hope could crawl
into the bottomless,
falling vastness of
sensing and proximity,

it would be here.

Moving in –
toward
and away –
from this this-ness is
the ever-mounting pulse
of the universal
call toward
echo-location and grace.

It rivals its own
simplistic ebbing and
flowing beyond the
beyond-ness to this.

Could there be a
THIS for all of the
miniscule and
grandiose particles and
waves of the

ONE THAT IS THAT.
"Tat tvam asi" is
under everything
that reverberates with
the scintillating
blueness of
creation and being.

Clear-light hides each
and every spec of the
eternal. A quark contains
a full cosmos, a
tachyon holds a whole
quasar. Can anyone
know the worth of anything
in this supermarket
of camouflage and
meaning.

Particles and Waves

Today I see the trees
on the edges of our land
with my eyes and
with my recollection.

The fog is so thick
it triggers my past notions
to fill in the gaps
of limbs

I can no longer
see; branches
of my most
recent memories.

The assumptions of my soul
rely upon familiarity
with the nerves on all
my skin –
across every inch
of me.

The immensity of
sensing is
under-known. The
connectivity of impression
is under-rated.

Every cell
takes its meaning and
worth from everything
it rubs against,
not just from
what it learns.

Without skin-sense
the hare is destined to

die again
and again.

Without feeling,
every thought would
fail to be born.

How is it
we have found our
skin repugnant
and turned ourselves
away from the cellular
nature of our
being.

Beauty Abrades the Harshness

If there is an antidote
to the harshness
that wells up
in the corners of the
unexamined life,

it is beauty.
The slanting,
early morning,
cool rays of the sun
expose an inquisitiveness
that somehow turns
to awe as I watch it dig
and claw its way to earth,
through the deep, dense vapor
of the morning cloud that sits
here on this mountain.

If not for this ten
small minutes in the
pool of early morning
stillness, I would have missed
a lifetime of beauty
reaching out for the tender and
ominous soil upon which
we all take our place.
What could my day have
become had not this
ravishing and glorious
beauty of an early morning
stellar drama taken away the
potential raspy harshness
that lies just below
the surface of our social and
political ways. For in them
we fight as if we were
left alone with only the

resources we have built
with feeble and myopic hands
and discontent. And yet,

an eye leaning into the
morning's light; an ear
leaning into the cicada's trill
forces away from us –
even for a breath
of an infinitesimal
instant of time –

the horrid dependency
on our own singular and
vacuous aloneness.

For an instant –

that instant –

beauty abrades the harshness
and a stillness enters
that saves us from our own
undoing and shame.

Tiny Waterfall in Jim Thorpe, PA

What Mark; What Groove

What mark is marked
upon this path of life;
what groove is grooved
into this crenulation of
my living. Can I turn
behind and simply
find what has been.

Can I look ahead
and see what is next
to come. Can I look to the
left and see all
those factors that will
mitigate themselves into
a faded tapestry
of meaning and
dependence –
a disappearing mural
of grit and grace.
Can I look to the
right and see all
that will blend
itself into my
becoming of my
own origin
and ash.

Swimming in Rivers

Swimming in
rivers and night-time
dreams has
eroded the danger
and the anger
from my heart;
taken it from
the places
under my nails.

The muddied
tributaries and
rivulets have
fed
and carried
the distribution
of all that has
needed to have
been persuaded
to leave.

It is what the hero
prays for atop
of the mountain
of his unbridled
conversion –

on the
long Herculean way
of his maturation and
despair; on the long
Promethean way
of his woundings and
healings.

His challenges
have been

met and exceeded
a thousand,
thousand
times as he
establishes
his supremacy
and grit.

His entrails have
been sown back
into his gut
a thousand,
thousand times
as the ravens
have pecked
themselves into
his core.

All of it
has washed away
with the dirt and
cinders the birds
had left behind.

These things
wear down
the edges of the
danger and the
anger that
have taken root
in a young man's
heart. Things that
have been planted
by his perception of
abandonment
and isolation.

These seeds

are really
known –
known
throughout the land –

as the growing
up of independence
and self-worth.
They are not
avoidable machinations
from a lack of integration
and support;
they are the way
any young
man must go.

Swimming in
rivers and night-time
dreams has
eroded the danger
and the anger
from my heart;
taken it from
the places
under my nails.

The muddied
tributaries and
rivulets have
fed
and carried
the distribution
of all that has
needed to have
been persuaded
to leave.

A Darkness Is Born

A darkness is born
in the heart
when a seed
of self-obsession
is given full
light and rain
enough
to grow itself
into more than a
sheltering shade.

It grows itself
out beyond the limits
of its own nature.

A darkness
darker than the
empty upside
down word.
The underside of
something you thought
you had understood.

A darkness of
character and
dismay.

It can envelop the
particles and hide the
waves of light
in a fashion that
can be mistaken
as a gentle
covering or a
soft enshrouding.

It's a choking darkness –

A Darkness Is Born

unable to allow
a breath to escape.

When you set out
into the deepness of
the dark, there is
a stillness replete
with calm
and a syncopated
rest; a repair
and undivided
repose. At the edges –

on the first dismal
shores of encounter and
and engagement.

What
lolls you in
is this –

the harsh wrestling
difference that
is posed by something
other than what is;

something that seems
against all that is.
In the end,
after
everything settles down,

we see that everything
remains and everything
is the One.

Darkness turns to light;
light turns to darkness. And
each is able to
lure you into
raptured guessing
at meaning and
position.

But,
without the anguish
that turns
to a steady
and rhythm-ed
familiarity of
what fear is built
up of, there can be
no knowing of the
value of the darkness
that is in our core. The
darkness that
is our very light. It is
just this side of that.

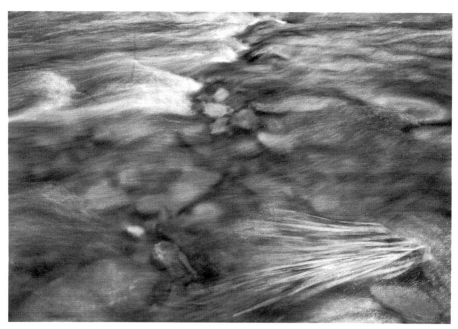

Tohickon Creek BW

There Is A Seed Of Emptiness

There is a seed
of emptiness in

the center of my
me; in the core
of our all.

Sitting there,
it pulses
and tries to find
a thing it can grab
hold of;
listening
to hear the sounds
that will set it free
from its own inability
to smelt its weight
and meaning from
all it sees and
knows to be solid
on the landscape of
worth and being.

It is not boredom
or a seeming apathy
of grandeur and wonder.
It is a hollow ring
so loud it deafens
us to what it is we hear

in the absence of
chaos and noise.

The Haunting Memory

The haunting memory
of some yonder, forgotten
melody, and the longing
chords of yearning from
just beyond the body

soak into me –

a lap steel guitar
whining its pained
lament into my soul

into my shoes as
I walk the path
back in and through
the woods of the
red shale foothills
rising up along
the banks of the Delaware

that had obscured his
anguish and filled him
with ease.
We learn that there is
some thing we cannot
hold, some me that is not
here strictly for
the eye to see.

His ashes are here

all among the lichen
and mosses that have
draped themselves over
the rocks and loam
of this earth-skin

on which I stand.

This time of writing
comes as it wills.

I have no clear means
to provoke the muse
or lure her here.

I cannot
hold sway over her;
making her to wander
this way and then that –
a puppeteer with a randy
disposition.

A gentle falling snowflake
of unusual shape and size;
a lilting piece of moss
draped carelessly over
a lichen covered rock.

These are instants that
push open the gates
of time-less-ness and
usher in the full now;

she follows in
just before
the door is closed.

I have no warning of
what sight will fire out
into the tangles of synapses
of the pictures in my mind;

I cannot foretell what
sound will reach back
and in to the registry
of interior rhapsody and song.

The Haunting Memory

The gray shroud
that hangs just at the
edges of this winter
mountain view
evokes a melody of
him; a sonata of
his presence.

Is it that his middle
name was Grey; or that
his sullen quiet nature
is in the pall of
cold and cloudy
mountain skies?

Does the marking –
one more time –
of his death
propose a banging
on the drums of
my remembrance;

the playing of the
O so ancient chords
of the familiar?

How can the muse
weave so rich and
warm a meaning
with
so few and fragile
strands of imagery –

fleeting and just
beyond our reach;

as if growing each
from seed herself.

It is on the premise
of this creative soil
that the muse
can plant, and tend,
and harvest the cotton
and the flax of
our very own cloth
of constitution – a
singularly
crafted self with her
own will to
arrive and begin work
as she like.

Tremont Creek, TN

I Know

I know you
can feel it –
the inner
twisted knot
that turns.

I know
you can
feel it
because
I do, too.

I know
you can
carve out the
words
to give voice
to it –
the dank
intermittent

horror
that you suppose.

I know
you can
carve them
because
I can, too.

It is really
more about
whether we
will allow
what is in there
to come up
and out.

I Know

I know you
have had it
eating at your
soul as you
sleep, work,
drive your car,
and look upon all
that is good
and sweet in your
children;

in the little
ones who have
not asked to
be born into
this slowly
eroding planet.

I know
it is eating
at your soul
because it eats
at my
soul, too.

But,
will you ever
let yourself
wail in public,

lament aloud
in your
temples, or
scream from
what is left of
the richness
of the soil

upon which
we all stand –

what we have
grown to
love as earth.

How can
you not;
how
can I not?

In the end
we must.

It is no longer
all about us,
it is about
all
that is good
and sweet in our
children.

It is
their home
we stand on,
now.

A Paper Ring

The frailty of
the examined
life is a sure thing.

Slipping in and
out of its delicate
wandering weave,
we are learning
to make and wear
a paper ring –

a sometime thing.

The filigree and
wispy edges betray
the passing nature
of this temporary
adornment of sorts;

an idea more
at home with
wishful thinking –

familiar again and
again and again
with the lacquer of
longing notions and
ambivalent aspirations.

Never quite solid enough
to be sure and
never quite sturdy
enough to last.

Pretty while it
endures; it is
only here

long enough to peak
our sense of
watchfulness
and attention
to its tending and
hermetic protection.

One movement this
way could tear it. One
movement that way
could fold it in two.
Then what do
you have left, but
a forgotten perfection
of detail and degree.

It takes a lifetime
to learn to shelter
so small and weak
a thing as joy;

it takes a gale of
focus to keep that
thing safe against
all chaos and dis-ease.

Draw in every fiber
of your intent; bring
together ever strand
of your desire and
mark out the boundaries
all around the stuff
that you need to keep
awe and beauty, wonder
and amazement just at
the tips of your fingers –

hidden in the moisture
of your every breath.
Without such food,
the soul is left abraded
by the elements of daily
grind - the warp and
weft unraveled against
a panoply of undoing
and confusion.

It takes all we have
to make a sometime
thing last against

all odds.

Great Holes of Forgetting

There are huge
places of forgetting –

not only in our lives,

but in the vast
fabric of all that
is – in the crenulations
of the universe herself.

A lingering knowledge
that we have more
to say; a pause to bring
forth something long ago
tucked away in the flash of
an instant, the passing
of the moment. These

black holes of human
consciousness stand in
their own depths
immeasurable and unfathomable
to that simple speck
of awareness – that
point in time and space
that knows it is a knowing.

How we threw the ball
on the front lawn, how we
played cards in the fort outback;
walking the streams in the
early morning mist looking
for furs to sell for cash –

these are the fragments
that flow in a backwash
from my soul.

Great Holes of Forgetting

But,
just beyond the river
of things remembered
are segments of a life
that fade out of view
into a black hole of
insurmountable size.

There is no longing that
calls them forth from the
depths of forgetting and
gives them to see
the light outside the pit
of frozen synapses.

I long to lay aside
the frustrated muscle of
searching through the
ebb and flow of all I
have known and known I know.

I beckon them to come
to me – to make a
singular showing so
I can turn the motor of
memory off; or, at least
let it idle melodically at
a low-grade hum
of steady remembrance.

There is no letting
go of the desire to tug
at impressions against the
constant, endless, relentless
pull of gravity.

This anomaly of the astronomy
of our lives may be a theorem

of probability, an equation
of the science of space and
time, but in my self

there is no doubt
about its elusive
placement, just outside
the limits of my
perception and ken.

O lonely movement
of discovery, give back to me
the things I know to have
known. O chasm of neural
space and time, shake loose
the things that were my
meaning then – and give

me rest.

Release the wrenching
of this un-circumscribable
singularity against my ability to
hold tight the dear, lost
pieces of my me.
All that steadies
the who of who
I am – living into
the expansion of all
that is wrestles against
the apparent entropy
of this event horizon
of my own being.

Tumbling Falls DWG

Up To My Knees In Me

There is a wearing down
that comes to my me
as I stand knee-deep
in a stream and cast out
over my right shoulder
into the deep and moving
waters. It is the wearing
down I love the most.
I release the digital
apparatus my brain has
merged with in the daily
grind of life in this modern
age of speed, agility and
robust communication. I am
set free to communicate with
my own me. My heart listens
to the structured dissolving of
my me into the nature of my
earthy wet surroundings.

I become the splash
and the ripple;
I become the hawk
and the screech.
I become the sun
and the cloud;
I become the wind
and the aroma of tall grass.

When I stand this
deep in the river I know
the place from which
the scops of old sang
their songs and lore.
Taliesin became a
trout and stag
with little effort

or suspension of
belief. You cannot
not feel yourself
take on the space
of all you feel and see.

The me I felt I
knew is not the me
I feel myself become;

you can not be a
human without losing
yourself to another
form – at least once.

Falling to the river
bed I am become the
moss and weeds gracefully
blowing in the downward
pull of the water's call and
gravity of motion.
I am the Mayfly awaiting
being consumed. I am the
quiver of the fish as it
strikes the line. These little
dyings are nothing in the
grand scheme of all I have
become; Rumi was right –
"What have I ever lost
from dying."

The sun dips
slowly behind the
stand of trees on
the far shore
and I feel the air
turn quickly toward
its falling. The night

is a ways off,
but you can feel
its steady approach.

Everything has a
rhythm to its expansion
and contraction. Can I wear
down the me I think I am
enough to feel it as the me
that is becoming?

All I Thought I Owned
for the Haitian survivors of the earthquake

Everything around me
is nothing but
crushed pieces of all
our lives –
piled high on
top of itself.

All I thought I
owned is worth less than
hay, wood, and stubble.
For those things I could
find a use; for these things
– here – I cannot.

How,
how do I begin to
fathom a world built on
such useless, putrefied
debris? I stand on the
same familiar, foreign soil
of Job. I am afflicted
with the same disparate
image of my own
dismantled self.
Those things I knew
as me; that made my
me are gone.
And, I am left with
a gaping tear in my
soul.

My family and
friends lost –
taken by
the quake

and rubble, disease and
a quickly arising
despair.
The ones who
died a swift death
to a wall or ceiling
are despised by those
who lie about in
this lingering
languishing and
wasting.

When shall I be saved
from the horror
that stalks me
at noonday
and captures
me at dusk?

I am able to
find no relief in
sleep – I pray all day
for death and death
does not come.

The grandeur of
the Pleiades and God's
storehouse for the rain
can only sustain my
angst for a fading
moment – chamomile buds
baked in the noonday sun;
the wafting aroma of
lavender on the bumble
bee wing.

I have only the peace
that lives between each

moment and some
of that is shared
with a fear of
the earth's hunger
to consume me at another
turn. How did the
simplicity of joy
fall apart at the shaking
of the ground? I pray –
with salt-laden tears
that splash upon
my dirty flesh –
that hope would
wend itself my way –
carried on the
feathery bristles
of the pappus of
new life.

Cascade of Slid 4, NY

The Smoothing

There is an undoing
that is not against
the growing of
tendrils and roots.

A smoothing
of the edges of
it all.

A sloughing off of
the dead cells
of atrophy and
bitter disregard.

A convoluted
but undisguised
carrying away
of all that is
not given
to the supple
and tender warmth
of needful things.

Even the icy
river knows
the warmth
of needful things.

I watched myself
coil up around my
own gritty intolerance
of a stranger
and the path they
choose to be
their own across
this trackless
land of life.

This is not a
needful thing.

This shard
of glass
under my nail
needs gone.

The bank exposed
by the mighty torrent
seems rough
and indisposed toward
grace and the finer
things of this colossal
life of repeated and
fathomless mercy.

But time, oh the
winds and sands
of abrasive time will
smooth the jagged
edges – exposing rock
and root for the
endless eyes of our
watching. Even
against all will.

The rounding
of things makes them
less work. Sandstone
becomes easier to
look at.

We find the rest
in abraded places –

a laying aside of
our parasympathetic

drive to integrate
conflict into safety;

a downgrading
of our desire to flee.

I have seen great logs
move down and away
from their knotted nests
of chaos and upheaval
along the river's path.

Tangles beyond the
touch of understanding
have been untied;
released their way
to go into the night of
turbulent flotsam and
unleashed angst.

But then,
there is
always more.

Can I survive the
aging of my sons
without losing too,
too much of my
incomplete joy
to the worries and
woes of the subtle
dying of their youth?

Does a grizzly
grieve the innocence of the
aging of its cubs?

All at once

my wrestling
with this will end;
one strand of
it will give way
to a constant releasing
of the whole Gordian
conglomeration and mess
of emotion and desire.

I have seen it
a thousand, thousand
times against the
topography of
my own soul.

Fighting a thing –
long enough –

wearies the muscle
into a slumped
relaxation that pulls
it out and away
from the conflict.
In tiredness
it falls to the
ground as if
the battle itself
has enabled a retreat
that has saved its
life.

A soul grows
this way in
the abrading of all
it is. At the end
of the day it finds
beauty in what it
has become because it

The Smoothing

has learned to
release its hold.
Valleys fill in,
mountains wear
down; and, the
untold process of the
Waterfall Way is
a smoothing.

Make friends with
that smoothing.

Dunfield Creek 10, NJ

The True Test

Could it be
the true test
of the clarity
and worth of
a soul is
the suffering it
has survived.

Its ability
to stand
while broken.

It arrives in
whatever space
it inhabits
with no fanfare
or finger pointing.

It does not
seek to rise above
on the backs of
innuendo and
accusation.

Facing into the
horror, it braces
as if its eyes were
closed and pointed
to the winds of
severe change and
relocation. It
shall not
be moved.
Feeling the
blasts of what
is named
across its cheeks

and edges
of its ears.

It finds no need
for justifying
explanation
or a trivial
varnishing of
a thing.
A gargoyle
resting its
head in its
hands.

The wave has no
need of discourse,
the sun no need
of banter.
A stone is unmoved
by insults.

Resting in
the ever-present
idleness of being,

it does not
move to grow.

Its nourishment is
in the stillness
of self. In its
perch and
point of vantage
viewing-absorption
it is abraded by
the ripples of
suffering and woe
that have coursed

over its
"itness" and self.

An alchemy of
a solid affirmation

that everything belongs.

The dis-ingenuous-ness
of a rosy painted outcome
stands against the rawness
of reality that is true;
Job's friends
unable to stare into
the vacuous-ness of
the universe of pain.

Perhaps it means
this; or maybe it requires
that. Reaching out for
form where formlessness
rules the day.

Suchness is crafted
from the gathered
nuclei of tears

that have run along
the dirty face of agony
and abandoned hope.

We reach these places
in the chaos of
form.

Lean into these
undoings with
acknowledged wordlessness

and rampant indefinability.
The circumscribable
is uncircumscribed.

The heavy snow
sits months on end
above the ginseng seeds
and crocus bulbs
longing to find day.
The tearing away
of melting snow
washes the soil
with the gift of growth,
carrying winter
away in rivulets
of supple freshness
and the morning song
of birds.

I Think I Have Found

I think I have found
the me that is left
after the endless,
countless abrasions
of the suffering and
mirth of this life

is a smoothened
out old piece of what
was brought here
in the first place.

It is the me that loves
as much to walk
and read and write
and cook and make love
and sit and sit and sit
as had been here all along.
It is the one
by the fountain reading
the classics, it is
the one with head hung
backward over the rocks
listening into the cavity
of the roaring stream.

He has been here
but is now all the
better for having learned
that these simple likes
are more then that;

these ambling attractions and
desires of the human heart
I hold and nurture
deep in this chest
are laconic and lapidary

koans of existence carved
out in the aeons of my
days. They are more than whim
and fancy; they sing out
as implacable standards of
my me. Sing this song,
my soul, sing that
reaching in and finding
a gem of delight can
proffer more riches than
caravans of cash. Sing, my
heart, that glee and bliss
have found more wealth in you
than all could imagine. What is
left at the end of the day
of sadness is a sense a little
more keen, a heart a little
more refined toward its true wont
and wealth beyond measure –
joy. Simple glinting charm comes
only after we see the depths of
its lack. Grand elongations of
hospitality and grace are only
shadows left in their own
sensed absence. Sing, that when
a man sees it all carried away
he finds then a stillness that
betrays its true worth.

For this, for all this,
I sing at what I think
I have found, a place
among myself
a seat within my me.
Here resides in each souls'
center a mountain pass
of freedom and a canyon
of wonder and grand design.

I Think I Have Found

For, everything belongs;
even that which we only speak
of in absence by abrasion.
Shadows on the river
walls of constant change
and removal.

That which is no longer here
sits stalwart beside all we
still behold.

Everything belongs and leaves
its smoothening wear and gives us
to know that it is all in there –
quarks eternally nestled
by the quasars of empty mind.

In it all,
I think I have found
my me.

Tears The Eyes Cannot Cry

I am undone
by the tears the
eyes cannot cry;
held to
tightly by the
need to carry on.
A reserve
toward strength
and unbridled
unaffectedness
by the current of
the daily flow.
A river swells
beyond its banks
only so often;

other days it
runs heavy.
Coursing strongly
to its delta.

I am Having To Amble

I am having
to amble my way
slowly, slowly along
the river;

padding my way
through the disinterested
fog as it rolls and
blows about.

There is a shrouding
blindness that comes
with this clouding mist;

hiding mostly all
that should be in my
line of sight.

Where has it all
gone? What has
befallen the earth
I knew? Will it
emerge again at the
decimation of
this dragon's breath?

There is a keen
likeness

to my days in midlife.

Rendered unfamiliar
with terrain I so
desperately long
to remember; I plod
on hoping - always
hoping that my next

step will open my eyes;
that my next bend in
the road will make everything
once again clear.

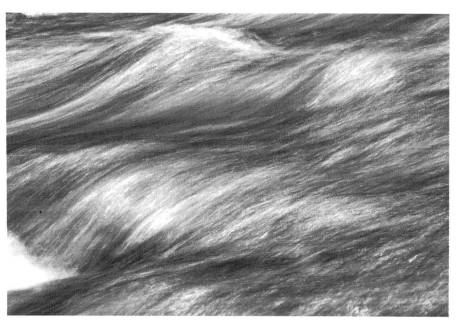

Waterflow 1